TESTIMONIALS

"This is like a mall-sized candy store of sweet, simple, easy-to-do information. I have used about every one of the steps Ellen mentions and can corroborate that her tips work well.

"One cool thing she does is tell you the tip-and then she tells you how to do it. Many tips books just leave you hanging without the step-by-step "how-to". There are lots of ideas and links to more resources than you can use in a year inside as well-from freebies to fee-based books you can get inexpensively on Amazon.

"Even though I'm familiar with these ideas, I shall keep this book by my side as I work on launching each of my books because I'll want to remember to do the easy stuff."

Angela Treat Lyon
Artist and Bestselling Author of Change Your Mind with EFT

"If you feel overwhelmed with trying to market your book, read this one and learn exact steps to doing it with ease and skill.

"It will help you launch your book successfully."

Tom Marcoux
Spoken Word Strategist
International Speaker
Author of over 47 books

21 SIMPLE STRATEGIES
TO JUMP START YOUR Book Marketing Online

PROVEN TECHNIQUES FOR QUICK RESULTS

ELLEN VIOLETTE

Create A Splash Publishing
Publisher's Data & Legal Information

©Copyright 2019
Create A Splash Publishing
All Rights Reserved

ISBN: 978-1-074590-05-5

Ellen Violette
info@booksbusinessabundance.com
www.booksbusinessabundance.com

This book may not be reproduced or transmitted in any form without the written permission of the publisher-or by any means-electronic, mechanical, photocopy, recording, scanning or other-except for brief quotations in critical reviews or articles, without prior written permission of the publisher.

Every effort has been made to make this book as accurate as possible. And while it has been prepared with great care, we assume no responsibility or liability for errors, inaccuracies or omissions.

The book is for educational purposes only. The author and publisher do not warrant that any information contained within is fully complete and shall have neither liability nor responsibility to any person or entity with respect to any loss or damage caused or alleged to be caused directly or indirectly by this book, nor do we make any claims or promises of your ability to generate income by using any of this information.

DEDICATION

For every author who has had the courage to write a book,
but had no clue how to start marketing it.

ACKNOWLEDGEMENTS

I want to acknowledge Eric Lofholm for believing in me and trusting me to help his clients finish their books from his Book-in- a-Day Program.

I figured as long as I was there, I might as well write another book, and that's how *21 Simple Strategies to Jump Start Your Book Marketing Online* was born.

To my community of authors who look to me to lead the way on writing, publishing, launching and marketing bestsellers and impacting their businesses with books.

And to my husband, who loves me unconditionally and supports me always.

TABLE OF CONTENTS

Terminology xi

Introduction 1

Strategy #1. The Guerilla in the Room – Amazon 5

Strategy #2. Oh Say Can You See (Getting Seen on Amazon) 7

Strategy #3. Double Your Book Profits Without Writing Another Word. 15

Strategy #4. Give it Away! 17

Strategy #5. The 10% Rule 19

Strategy #6. Put Your Book Front and Center 25

Strategy #7. Add it to your John Hancock 27

Strategy #8. Read All About It 31

Strategy #9. Assemble a Book-Review Team 35

Strategy #10. Let Others Brag About Your Book! 39

Strategy #11. Be a Podcast Guest Speaker 41

Strategy #12. Blog It! 45

Strategy #13. Repurpose It 47

Strategy #14. Tweet It! 53

Strategy #15. The Answer Is…..
(Answer questions on discussion boards) 55

Strategy #16. Chat About it! 57

Strategy #17. Let Your Fingers Do The Walking
(Put your book in eBook/PDF Directories) 61

Strategy #18. Comments Please! 63

Strategy #19. Pin it! 65

Strategy #20. The 30% Switch 69

Strategy #21. Discount it! 73

Resources 75

Next Steps 81

About Ellen Violette 83

TERMINOLOGY

Amazon refers to the company and website of the company.

Amazon books generally refer to physical books.

Kindle books are digital books (ebooks), and Kindle is the digital book division of Amazon.

KDP refers to Kindle Direct Publishing for publishing on Amazon in digital form.

KDP Select refers to a free launch or promotion in Kindle.

Countdown refers to a discounted launch or promotion in Kindle.

Launch refers to a new book's coming out.

Promotion refers to a relaunch of an existing book if you already launched it.

INTRODUCTION

When I got online in 2004, I knew nothing about direct-marketing copywriting or marketing online. All I knew was that I wanted to write books, so I got online and quickly discovered ebooks. I loved the idea of writing them because you could write and publish almost instantly, and you could get directly to your audience and make good money doing it. (In those days, Kindle didn't exist; we sold ebooks directly from a website, and they sold for $27 or more!) But what attracted me to ebooks was that you didn't have to write a book proposal, face rejection letters, or wait two years for your book to get published.

So, I started writing my first one, and when I realized I needed help, I went looking for an ebook coach. In the meantime, I started listening to free webinars online and attending in-person conferences where I heard over and over that the money was not in the books but in the back-end.

In those days, THE conference to attend was The Big Seminar with Armand Morin. I thought that would be the perfect place to find an ebook coach. But, I was shocked to find that there weren't any. That's when I decided, it could be a good fit for me. So, I found a coach who taught me how to coach, and I created my first signature workshop.

In the first few months, I built a list of about 200 people; it was slow. But, then I heard about a bonus giveaway with the late Mark

Hendricks. He enlisted over seventy entrepreneurs, coaches, and experts who each gave a bonus for the giveaway and cross-promoted the event. I wrote an ebook that led to a two-part training on how to write an ebook and grew my list to over 1600 people in just two weeks; I was instantly in business! Then, I upsold people into my first workshop. But, getting it up online was a nightmare. I had no tech skills, and, in those days, you had to know html. There was no way I would be able to get up to speed in time, so I hired help. I made about $47,000 my first year and almost all of it went to my team.

I only got two people into that first workshop; I was devastated. But, once I taught it and got feedback on the flaws, I was grateful that I only had two people in it. I continued to give it and improve it and have now taught it thirty times as of the time of publishing this book.

After the first workshop, my subscribers asked me to create a marketing workshop. The challenge was that I knew there were topics that needed to be covered that I did not know enough about to teach. So, I enlisted help. Mari Smith, Facebook expert, taught email marketing, Paul Colligan, podcasting expert, taught affiliate marketing, and Craig Perrine taught list building.

Next, I tackled creating a summit. Mind you, this was 2007 when very few people were doing them. It was called the Virtual eBook Expo, and again, I leveraged the expertise of others and made $16,000 and $20,000 on the first two, and I continued to hone my skills and improve my workshops and turn them into home-study programs.

But, along the way, everything changed and my third Expo lost money. But about that time, Wordpress websites and blogs appeared, and social media changed the way we market and sell; and, of course, Kindle was born, which revolutionized publishing. And while the tools became easier to use, there were so many more ways to market and so much more information telling us about the newest strategy, software, or program that we just HAD to have to be successful. And believe me, I tried them all! And what I finally realized was that the best thing to do was actually to do less and simplify my marketing.

But, these changes in the marketplace have led too many authors, entrepreneurs, coaches, and independent professionals and speakers to an epidemic of information overload and analysis paralysis. I talk to so many who are overwhelmed and unsure of what to do to market their books and their businesses, who are stuck in their heads trying to figure out what will get them where they want to go the fastest, and what will be the easiest for them to implement-wondering if it will work, if it will make them any money, and if it's worth it to even try. And that's why I've put together this book, *21 Simple Strategies to Jump Start Your Book Marketing Online, Proven Techniques for Quick Results.*

My goal is to stop you from spinning your wheels and start taking action IMMEDIATELY with proven strategies that are easy to implement. No more guessing, no more worrying about what to do first or next and how to do it. These are simple techniques that will get you out of overwhelm and help you market and sell more books with ease.

STRATEGY #1

THE GUERILLA IN THE ROOM — AMAZON

Publish your book on Amazon. Amazon is the largest seller of books in the U.S. including self-published books and ebooks, so it's crazy NOT to publish your book(s) there. If you can afford to format your book in both PDF and ePub for physical and digital books, do both. But, if not, start with a digital book as they are cheaper to produce, faster to publish, and easier to promote. (eBooks usually take about four to six hours to publish, although Amazon warns authors it could take up to twenty-four hours while physical books may take up to seventy-two hours or longer.)

Another reason to publish in Amazon is that Amazon has some great promotional tools to help you jump start your marketing and create buzz by promoting your book as an ebook in KDP (Kindle Direct Publishing). This service is especially helpful to new authors who do not have a list and/or much of a reach in social media. It is also a good way to create momentum to sell books for all authors. (I'll explain in more detail later.) And, it's FREE to use!

To publish your book in paperback and ebook formats, go to www.kdp.amazon.com to get started.

STRATEGY #2
OH SAY CAN YOU SEE (GETTING SEEN ON AMAZON)

Amazon sells millions of books, and those that sell are the ones that are the most visible-that means they appear on the first page for any keyword search for relevant terms for that topic. (No one can buy your book if they can't find it!) So, you want your book to appear on the first page.

In order to achieve this goal, you have to do the research to find the best keywords and categories for your book. That way, your book will appear each time a potential buyer searches for books on your topic.

Note: Amazon lets you submit seven keywords and two categories. If you want more categories you have to contact them and ask for more at: kdp-support@amazon.com

So, how do you do the research?

Start by making a list of the main keywords people would probably look for if they were looking for my book. Don't overthink it; just start writing and add as many as you can.

Let's say your topic were "spiritual awakening"

Your list might include words like:

>   connect to spirit
>   spirit
>   spirituality
>   spiritual awakening
>   spiritual rebirth
>   consciousness
>   personal development etc.

Once you've compiled your list, go to Wordtracker.com and look up each of the words to see which ones get the most traffic. You can change the time frame and the location. I generally use "monthly" and "United States".

For example, When I enter "connect to spirit", this is what comes up:

>   clairvoyant 90,500
>   card reader 18,100
>   spiritual awakening 14,800
>   and the volume gets smaller as you go down the list from there.

If "clairvoyance" or "card reader" are not related to what the book is about, then what you look at is "spiritual awakening" at 14,800 volume, since that is the topic. (Volume is not exactly the same as clicks, but you can see how each word or phrase stacks up against the other phrases to give you a good idea of which words and phrases will pull in the most traffic.)

On further evaluation, you can see that "spiritual awakening" is in that search, so pick another one, like "spirit".

This is what comes up:

> spirit airlines
> spirit
> spirited away
> sprint phones
> us airways
> spirit com

As you can see, some of these words are completely unrelated; ignore those. But, "spirit" gets a volume of 1,000,000 in volume. Next, you have to figure out what people could be looking for when they look up "spirit". However, you have to discern whether you think enough of those are looking up the kind of spirit that we are looking for or if they were looking up airplane abbreviations. And even if they do mean spirit the way we mean it, it's generic, so it makes sense that it would have a huge volume. But, at least, it lets us know that people are interested in "spirit"!

Next, look up "spirituality". Here's what comes up:

> Yoga 450,000
> Jesus 301,000
> meditation 201,000
> God 201,000

Christian 165,000
Psychic 135,000
religion 110,000
metaphysics 110,000
mystic 74,000
spirituality 60,500

Look at the list and see which of these words make sense for the book you are thinking about writing. Copy down the volume for each and go on to your next word, until you have researched at least 5-10 of them.

In this case, you may want to use some of the words that appear with higher volume than spirituality IF they are pertinent. If not, "spirituality" still has a volume of 60,500 volume, so it is big enough to pursue.

Note: Wordtracker is free, but gives you a limited number of searches per day. If you want to look up more than the allotted words for free searches, you will either have to pace yourself over a few days time or upgrade to a paid account.

Once you know which of your relevant keywords get the most volume, go to Amazon and put each of the ones you are considering in the search bar, one at a time.

First, look to see how many books come up for that search. (If there are only a few books, it's not a good topic. If there are millions, then it's a very popular topic, but competitive, which is not necessarily bad. However, if you don't have great marketing chops, it's better to find something in between.)

Next, look to see if there are any bestsellers on the page. Bestsellers have a banner above the book cover and/or under the name of the book and looks like this (This is from a book launch we did for *Niche Down*):

> by Christopher Lochhead ▾ (Author), Heather Clancy ▾ (Author), & 1 more
> ☆☆☆☆☆ ▾   19 customer reviews
> #1 Best Seller in Small Business
>
> › See all 2 formats and editions
>
> | Kindle | Paperback |
> | --- | --- |
> | $0.00 kindleunlimited | $14.69 ✓prime |

Bestsellers show you that books on that topic, using that keyword you are searching for, have the potential to be a bestseller. If there are multiple bestsellers, all the better; if there are no bestsellers, it may not be the best keyword. But, if using that keyword makes the best title, you may use it in your title, and then use other better keywords in your subtitle for Amazon SEO or use them in your seven keywords for publishing.

Next, look at the ranking. There are two types of ranking: 1. The overall Amazon ranking called *Amazon Best Sellers Rank*. That is the ranking of the book in relation to all the other books in Amazon. 2. The ranking for each category that it ranks for, which shows the ranking number. So, if it were #1 In the category, it would say #1, and then show you the path to the final category. Amazon ranks each book within each category. And, you only have to get to #1 in a category to have a #1 bestseller, not in all of Amazon.

Here's an example; you can see in the "Product Details" for my #1 Bestseller, *How to Crush it in Business Without Crushing Your Spirit, How Entrepreneurs Can Overcome Depression and Find Success* below, the path to get into the Decision-Making and Problem-Solving category is as follows:

>Kindle eBooks
>Business & Money
>Management & Leadership
>Decision-Making & Problem solving

Product details
File Size: 2177 KB
Print Length: 143 pages
Publication Date: December 7, 2017
Sold by: Amazon Digital Services LLC
Language: English
ASIN: B075MPZKP9
Text-to-Speech: Enabled
X-Ray: Not Enabled
Word Wise: Enabled
Lending: Enabled
Screen Reader: Supported
Enhanced Typesetting: Enabled
Amazon Best Sellers Rank: #522 Free in Kindle Store (See Top 100 Free in Kindle Store)
   #1 in Kindle Store > Kindle eBooks > Business & Money > Management & Leadership > **Decision-Making & Problem Solving**
   #1 in Kindle Store > Kindle eBooks > Business & Money > Entrepreneurship & Small Business > **Entrepreneurship**
   #58 in Kindle Store > Kindle eBooks > **Nonfiction**

The way you get to #1 is by outranking the book that is #1 at the time that you are doing your launch or promotion. There are two lists for each category: free and paid. If you are doing a free launch, then you have to beat out the #1 free book, and if you are doing a paid launch, then you have to beat out the #1 paid book. Obviously, it is easier to get to #1 with a free promotion than a paid one, but both have their benefits, which I'll discuss later.

You can find out the overall ranking of any #1 book by clicking on the category, finding the #1 book under it, and then going to the sales page for that book and checking out it's ranking. (That is the book you will have to beat.)

To make it easier to keep track, create a worksheet. List your main keywords and categories at the top. Then, as you go through the keywords searches, list each title, and copy and paste in their overall ranking and category ranking, so you can compare your finding once you have gone through all your main keyword searches.

For my Kindle Planner, How to Position your eBook on Kindle to become a #1 Bestseller and Sell more Books, go to: http://www.books-businessabundance.com/kindleplanner

STRATEGY #3

DOUBLE YOUR BOOK PROFITS WITHOUT WRITING ANOTHER WORD

It's easy to double your profits by formatting your book in both PDF and ePub. Once you do, you can use "Matchbook" in KDP. This allows book buyers to get the Kindle version immediately with the purchase of the paperback either for free, for 99 cents or for $1.99 -depending on your preference.

And while it's easier to promote your book using the ebook, there will always be a certain number of potential buyers who prefer the book. By offering your book in both formats, you will capture those who want the digital version, those who want the physical book, and those who want both. Plus, if you charge for the digital version, it can add up to a tidy extra profit stream!

Note: Whether you decide to charge for the Kindle version or not- if you are using Matchbook-depends on your target market and how you, and they, feel about the extra charge. It will also depend on if you are more interested in getting your information out to more people or making more money. Obviously, you'll get more takers if it's free. Plus, buyers will be more apt to feel warm and fuzzy if they get the digital version at no cost, but if your market is high-end, they may see even $1.99 as a big bargain while not diluting the value of your work.

To format your book for free, go to:

>http://ellenlikes.com/ebookstyles
>www.jutoh.com
>www.calibre-ebook.com
>www.smashwords.com

To use the best templates/software, go to

>Book Design Templates
>http://ellenlikes.com/bookdesigntemplates *

>Designr
>http://ellenlikes.com/designr *

To have it done for you, go to:

>www.booksbusinessabundance.com/services

>(We include inside design and have 100% success rate getting our authors to #1 who hire us to do their covers and inside design for physical and digital books when they use our bestseller system.)

If you're on a tight budget, you can find someone at: www.fiverr.com

---

Signifies that it is an affiliate link and I will make a commission if you use my link, which I appreciate.

STRATEGY #4
GIVE IT AWAY!

Launch your book with a free KDP Select giveaway to be visible, create buzz, become a #1 bestseller, gain momentum for book sales, get new prospects and make a bigger impact almost instantly! (If you set your book up right as I explained in strategy #2, it should not be hard to get to #1.)

I prefer to start with a KDP-Select free launch for two reasons, (if your book has already been published, you can do a promotion at any time as long as you give Amazon the ninety-day exclusive):

1. There are over 100 places where you can announce your upcoming launch. Many of these sites have thousands or even hundreds of thousands of subscribers, so you don't need an email list to reach a large audience! Plus, the books are listed by topic, so you get TARGETED traffic. These are potential customers you would not have reached otherwise. And if you set your book up properly, a proportion of them will get on your subscriber list, and the money is still in the list (your email subscriber list).

   Plus, you don't even have to do it yourself. My team knows the very best places to announce your book for maximum visibility and to give you the best chance to become a #1 bestselling author.

Contact us for a quote at: https://booksbusinessabundance.com/services/

2. Coaches, speakers, and experts give away free information all the time to get people to opt into their subscriber list, yet many authors don't like the idea of giving their books away for free. But, the truth is that you get in front of more people and get more people to download your book if it's free, (And, a percentage of them will read your book and want to take the next step, so you make money on the back end.)

Plus, the beauty of KDP free launches is that you can only give your book away from one to five days in any ninety-day period-so it's not like you're giving it away forever. It's just to jump start the process, make you a #1 bestselling author and make a big splash!

Note: We generally do two days free because we have seen a large drop off on the third day of a free launch. However, it may depend on which days of the week you give your book away. We have also seen that five day launches work well for fiction although our focus is on non-fiction books.

In one study, it showed that Sunday and Monday get the most traffic. So, if your goal is to get the most downloads for free, you'll want to give it for free on Sunday and Monday and do a five-day launch. But, KDP Select launches can go from one to five days and can be broken up any way you want to use them.

Go to www.kdp.amazon.com to get started.

STRATEGY #5
THE 10% RULE

Even though you must give Amazon/Kindle a ninety-day exclusive on your book to take advantage of these promotions, you may give away 10% of your book on any other sites. This allows you to give people a "taste" from your blog or website, a short podcast, or video, and encourages them to purchase your book. The way to do this is to put a call to action at the end of the teaser with your link to your book in Amazon, so it guides them to your sales page on Amazon.

If you don't have a website yet, I suggest setting one up using WordPress. I tried to set mine up directly from their site when I first starting using WordPress and found it too difficult to do, but if you want to try it, go to www.wordpress.org

 An easier solution is to sign up for hosting at Hostgator. http://ellen-likes.com/besthosting4u * Once you sign up, you can use the "Quick Install" feature and set it up in just a few minutes;

Instructions:

Go to your Cpanel to the software section

The first icon on the upper left side is "Quick Install". Click on it.

It will take you to "Popular Installs"

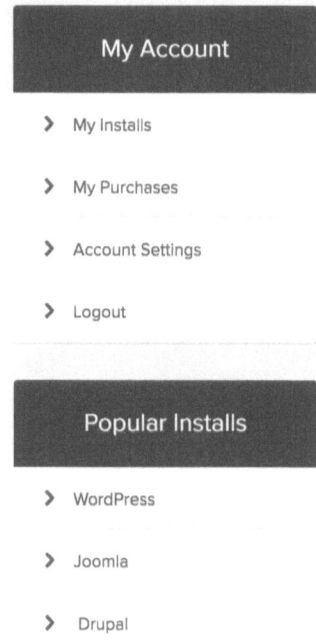

Click on "WordPress". Go to the Free Option and hit "Install WordPress"

Fill in the information below

The path will be the website URL

Admin email is where you want to receive information about the site going forward.

Username can be admin or your name. I don't recommend using your virtual assistant's name as that can change.

When you are done filling it out, hit "Install WordPress" and you're done!

Install WordPress

Fill out the form below to get started with your install.

[dropdown] / [install/path/here]

Admin Email
[   ]

Blog Title
[   ]

Admin User
[   ]

First Name
[   ]

Last Name
[   ]

[Install WordPress]
By clicking Install/Import above, you

If you still need help, a Hostgator technician can walk you through it. I suggest starting with the Premium Plan for under $6 a month.

Then, you can use a theme to create your pages quickly. I use Optimize Press. It comes with several templates that are already optimized for both computer and for mobile, and it is one of the most cost-effective and easy-to-use programs, once your learn the basics. You can purchase it at http://ellenlikes.com/optimizeitwow *

Or, if you want to jump in with an integrated solution, with an auto-responder function, automated websites and an affiliate program, I recommend Click Funnels at http://ellenlikes.com/clickfunnelsfree * They have a free 14-day trial. (I use both.)

They also have an excellent training challenge called The One Funnel Away Challenge, that gives you everything you need to know to succeed at creating offers that sells! http://ellenlikes.com/ofa *

If you decide to take it, send an email to ellen@BooksBusinessAbundance.com for a free funnel strategy session, a free+shipping funnel, and access to a private coaching group for extra support.

If you need help setting up Click Funnels, send an email to ellen@BooksBusinessAbundance.com Subject line: Click Funnels Help and we will connect you to our tech support team.

*This signifies that it is an affiliate link and I will make a commission from the sale.

STRATEGY #6
PUT YOUR BOOK FRONT AND CENTER

A really easy way to market your book is to mention it in your social media profiles. You can do this on your profile page on Facebook, Instagram, LinkedIn and any other sites you frequent.

You can also take a snapshot of the cover of your book or make a banner on your site to garner more interest.

I put together an anthology with sixteen co-authors called *How to Crush it in Business Without Crushing Your Spirit, How Entrepreneurs Can Overcome Depression and Find Success,* and I made a banner for the Facebook Group on the same topic at: www.Facebook.com/groups/overcomingdepressionforentrepreneurs

If you look closely, you can see the link to the book on Amazon under the book on the left, and then there is the invitation to join the group on the right.

STRATEGY #7
ADD IT TO YOUR JOHN HANCOCK

Add your book title to your email signature. This is a very easy way to get the word out to people about your book. The key is to write a catchy title and subtitle that tells your target audience the benefit of reading your book-so no explanation is needed.

In Gmail, you can add your book to your signature by following these instructions:

1. Click on the little wheel in the upper right-hand corner that looks like this:

2. In the drop-down menu, click on "settings"

> Try the new Gmail
>
> Display density:
> ✓ Comfortable
> Cozy
> Compact
>
> Configure inbox
>
> Settings
> Themes
>
> Get add-ons
>
> Send feedback
> Help

3. Go to "Signature"

And, add a signature or change a signature

This signature of mine advertises my book: *Turn Your Book into $10K Clients* at www.bookto10kclients.com It also includes how to connect with me in social media.

You can create more than one signature by using the arrow on the right-hand side of my signature.

STRATEGY #8
READ ALL ABOUT IT

If you put out a newsletter, a really easy way to promote your book(s) is to list them in your newsletter or to list the URL to the webpage where people can buy them.

If you don't have a newsletter, I suggest starting one. It doesn't have to be complicated, but it is a way to make sure that you touch base with your list at least once a week. (With so much noise in the market place, it's out of site out of mind, and consistency is important as well. Your subscribers want to know that you are not a flake.)

Putting out a newsletter on a regular basis also helps your subscribers to know you, like you, and trust you at a deeper level and can add additional sales to your bottom line.

I currently create my newsletter in Infusionsoft but I will be moving it in the future. I don't recommend it. Infusionsoft is complicated to use and Click Funnels is a much better option in today's marketplace. Another good option if you have more to spend is Constant Contact. www.constantcontact.com You can also create one in Click Funnels.

I include my books in each newsletter in the "Resource" section at the bottom of each one. It looks like this:

Resources

Books by Ellen Violette: www.BooksBusinessAbundance.com/books
Podcast: www.BooksBusinessAbundance.com/podcast/
Blog: www.BooksBusinessAbundance.com/blog

Free Videos www.YouTube.com/ellenviolette
Articles www.LinkedIn.com/in/ellenviolette
Free Videos, Articles & More at: www.EllenViolette.LinktoEXPERT.com

Notice that I listed my books on my website instead of on Amazon because not all my books are on Amazon at this time. (This is a good strategy if you want to sell some books for more than the going rate on Amazon.)

However, if all your books are on Amazon, you may list the Author Central URL instead of your website address in your newsletter.

If you don't yet have an Author Central Page, you can get started at: https://authorcentral.amazon.com/

If you already have one, you can find your URL by googling "Amazon Central (your name)"

Mine is: https://www.amazon.com/Ellen-Violette/e/B00BJQQSPK
My cloaked link is http://ellenlikes.com/amazoncentral

I use Easy Direct to cloak it, http://ellenlikes.com/prettylink * I like it because it is simple to use and when it comes to technology, I like simple!

Note: If you don't have a lot of books, or have one or two books that you want to highlight or that sell better than all the others, then you may want to list them by name instead in your newsletter, but you don't want a whole laundry list of books on your newsletter!

STRATEGY #9
ASSEMBLE A BOOK-REVIEW TEAM

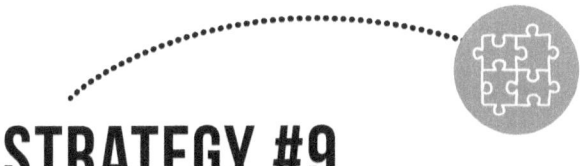

Book reviews sell books. The first thing consumers do when trying to decide if they want to buy a book or not is to read the reviews. Reviews let people know 1. if the book is popular and 2. if it's worth reading. Reviews can tip the scales on whether your readers buy or move on.

They are also important because of Amazon's algorithm. The more reviews you get, the more Amazon will help you promote your book. Getting thirty reviews or more greatly increases the amount of marketing Amazon will do for you.

Reviews are also very important for book launches. Announcement sites want to know that your book is worth promoting, so many require that you have at least four to six four and/or five-star reviews.

And the sooner you get these reviews, the sooner you can officially launch, the sooner you will start selling books!

The best way to line up reviews quickly is to put together a book-review team. These are people who agree to give you a review when your book goes live in exchange for a free copy in advance. You can also offer the book for ninety-nine cents before the official launch to get more people to purchase. Some may then give you a review.

But, just know even though they have good intentions, the truth is that many people will say they will write a review for you, but only a fraction of them actually will, so it's important to enlist enough people to get the reviews you need to jump start your marketing. The best way is to approach people who 1. You trust to follow through and 2. Love what you do and want to support you. This does not mean you cannot put out a general call for reviewers, just know your percentages will be lower if you do it that way.

WARNING: Amazon may ban you if you get reviews from family members, close friends and/or business associates with whom you make money or have a financial arrangement. Unfortunately, Amazon will not tell you when they remove a review, who it came from or which type of relationship they believe you have with that person. So, do not get reviews from people who share your last name, people who you have let inside your Amazon account or people you are connected to on Facebook if your Facebook is connected to your Amazon account through your phone or computer.

How to get reviewers:

1. Create an opt-in page on your website and invite people to get a free book in exchange for giving you a review.

2. Post in Facebook or on other social- media sites and let people know they will be able to get a free book if they want to review it.

3. You may also promote your free offer on other social-media sites and drive people to the Facebook post or your website.

4. Invite people to review your book one-on-one through Facebook Messenger.

5. Amazon reviewers

These are people who do write a lot of reviews on Amazon and their reviews are given more credence than other reviews. It is not necessary to get Amazon Reviewers to review your book, but it does add a nice touch and gives you a little extra credibility. Most Amazon reviewers only review in one or a few genres, so it's important to reach out to the right reviewers. And it takes some planning as it takes time to get them to see your request and decide if it's a fit for them, then actually write the review.

For my free guide go to: http://kickitwithkindle.com/amazon-reviewers/

Verified Reviews vs. Non-Verified Reviews

Verified reviews come from people who got the book on Amazon's site-either for free or by paying for it. Non-verified reviews are from free copies given away off of Amazon. Amazon gives more weight to verified reviews and to reviews from their reviewer list.

One way to get verified reviews is to give a free copy in advance, and then have the same people download the book for .99 when it goes live and then offer to pay them back.

STRATEGY #10
LET OTHERS BRAG ABOUT YOUR BOOK!

Testimonials, like reviews, are social proof. And while testimonials are technically different from reviews: a testimonial is a "written recommendation of worth" and a review is a "critical evaluation, they operate the same way. We generally call them reviews on third-party sites and testimonials on the back cover of your book and on websites.

Share your testimonials on your book website page and on book-sales pages on your site if you have any.

The best way to get reviews is to ask for them after someone has used a product, program, or service. One great way to do it is to give a follow-up call as a bonus with the purchase, get them on a video/audio call using a program like Zoom www.zoom.us.com or audio call using Instant Teleseminar at www.instantteleseminarsnow.com. You can introduce them and what they bought, then prompt them with questions like:

1. How did X work for you?

2. What challenges did you face and how did X solve the problem for you?

3. How easy was X to use?

4. How long did it take to complete X?

5. What would you tell other people who are thinking about ordering X?

You can find 9 cool testimonial templates at: https://boast.io/5-examples-of-testimonial-request-emails-that-work/

STRATEGY #11
BE A PODCAST GUEST SPEAKER

Podcasts are hot, and podcasters are always looking for interesting guests to interview on their shows. Look for shows that cover the topics in your book(s) so that you can mention your book on the show.

The best way to get on podcasts is to create relationships with podcasters in your niche. This can be done through social media. Do not ask to be on a podcast without building a relationship unless you use a podcast service or sheet that is specifically looking for guests or pitch on a "pitchathon". (Some podcasters, like Steve Olsher, occasionally do live shows where they invite you to pitch to big podcasts.)

The format for pitching for a podcast goes like this:

Step 1: Ask a question

    Did you know that….
    In other words, what's the problem that the market has

Step 2: Tell them how you solve the problem

    If you want X, you need Y

Step 3: Introduce yourself

>Hi I'm (Your Name) of (Your Company)
>Share your credentials
>What makes you unique/different
>Specifically how you help your market solve the problem.

Step 4: Action Step

>If you're ready to get started, you can get X at: www.…

Here are a few places to look for opportunities.

Two lists that I subscribe to for free are:

>http://myradioshowtour.com/ from Mark Bowness
>http://www.podcastguests.com from Andrew Allemann

Here's one more that I found that also looks promising:

>http://www.radioguestlist.com

Note: I have been on Steve Olsher's show and connected with one of his big podcasters. But, even if you don't get picked, they will help you tighten up your pitch. You can learn more at his site www.profiting-withpodcasts.com

Another good resource is Tom Schwab; he specializes in getting authors on podcasts. You can reach out to him at: Interviewvalet.com or tom@interviewvalet.com.

BTW: It's even easier to meet movers and shakers by creating your own podcast! Plus, it gives you a greater visibility and helps you make a bigger impact! I highly recommend it!. You can learn more about my podcast at: www.BooksBusinessAbundance.com/podcast And if you would like help getting started, you may sign up for a Quick 10-Minute Discover Session at: http://ellenlikes.com/scheduleconsult to see if we're a fit. I can help you design your podcast so that it dovetails with your book marketing.

Another resource you can check out if you are a do-it-yourselfer and you would like a free course on podcasting from my friend and colleague, Matt Johnson go to: http://pursuingresults.com/training

STRATEGY #12
BLOG IT!

Offer excerpts from your book on your blog. The easiest way to create book-marketing content for your blog is to lift pieces of content directly out of your book and use them as blog posts. Be sure to include a link to your book, so people can purchase it after reading the post.

You can also write blog posts about topics that you cover in your book. Go into more depth into specific topics and/or create checklists and step articles that help people consume enough of the information in your book to want more!

If you don't have a blog yet, some hosting sites give you a way to create a Wordpress blog inside their hosting.

To set up a blog, again, you can use Hostgator http://ellenlikes.com/besthosting4u (If you set up a WordPress site, you will automatically have a blog too!)

You can also guest post on other blogs that have influence in your niche.

Follow the influencer, get to know them, and offer value to their readers.

STRATEGY #13
REPURPOSE IT

Take your blog post and post it on LinkedIn To post in LinkedIn, go to your profile page in LinkedIn. At the top of the page, you will see the invitation to post. It looks like this:

Share an article, photo, video or idea

[Write an article] [Images] [Video]   **Post**

Click on "Write an article:

Add your headline here:

|Headline

Write here. Add images or a video for visual impact.

Then, copy and paste your article in below "Headline" where it says: "Write here. Add images or a video for visual impact"

Be sure to add a call to action at the bottom of your article to move your readers to the next step that you want them to take. I usually send people to my Facebook group at: www.Facebook.com/groups/selfpublishingcommunity unless I am writing about something that leads to a free lead magnet on my site or a Click Funnels funnel.

Also, add a picture to each article. Articles with pictures at the top of the page get more attention than those that do not Include a picture.

I get most of my graphics at www.123rf.com You can buy a pack of 40 credits for $39. When choosing your graphics, be sure to check how many credits it will take so you don't overpay. Also, get the small one, it's always the least expensive.

Tip: I take a snapshot of the photograph or graphic I am considering purchasing. It will have the watermark on it so you can't publish it. But, I use it to make sure it will work in the space allotted for my LinkedIn picture. Sometimes, I can size them and it works, other times I have to find a different graphic.

To size a graphic:

Click on the graphic

Self Publishing Community for Entrepreneurs
with Ellen Violette

Ellen Violette

Go to "Tools" in the tool bar

Preview   File   Edit   View   Go   Tools   Window   Help

Go to "Adjust the size"

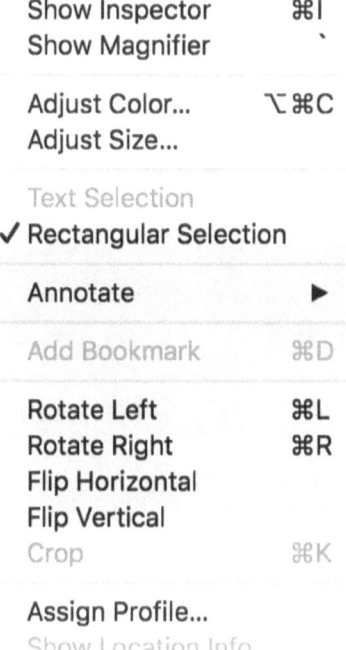

Click on it

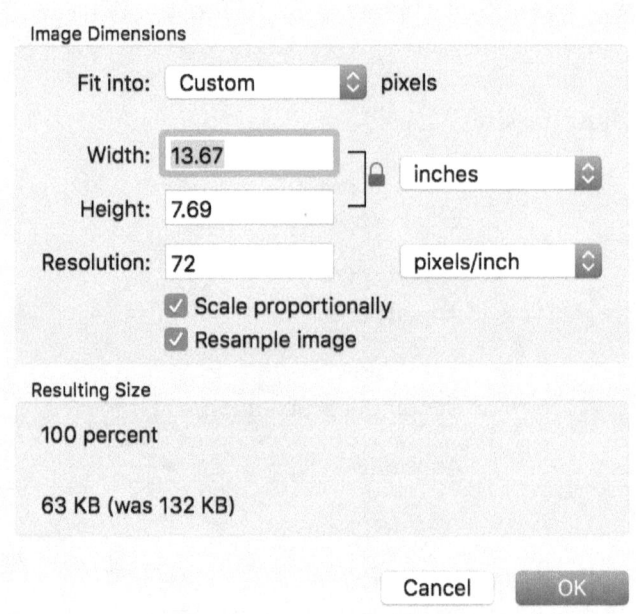

The picture size of the one I was sizing was 26+ so I took the width down to 13.67, and then the height automatically adjusted.

Click on the OK buttom and you'l have your newly sized photo.

If you want it smaller still, just adjust the width.

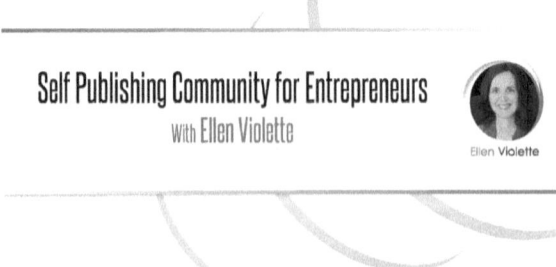

But, on a blog, the banner is laid out horizontally, so you'll want to find photographs and graphics that are laid out that way as well like this one of happy and sad faces.

Do not get graphics that are vertical like this one below:

Buying graphics can add up quickly, so also consider other ways to get graphics, including using a site like Canva.com where you can make your own for free. However, note, that some of their

Higher-end graphics cost $1 each. Canva is easy to use once you know how but there is a learning curve and they do not have good instructions, so I created a guide that you can purchase at: https://theebookcoach.com/canva-graphics

Also consider creating your own; it's easy to do with a smartphone, and the pictures are very high quality. You can even sell them at www.twenty20.com and make some extra income!

STRATEGY #14
TWEET IT!

Create a hash tag for your book. The way you do this is to add "#" and the word you want people to be able to find. Keep it short because you don't want to use up all your characters for your tweet on your hashtag—especially if you're not famous and most people don't know your book!

A hash tag is basically an abbreviation or what is called a "metadata tag" used to tag tweets, so others can easily find messages with a specific theme or content. The way you create a hashtag is by putting

The # sign or pound sign in front of a word or phrase in or at the end of a message .

Here are two of the hashtags for my books to give you some ideas:

Turn Your Book into $10K Clients, 5 Keys to a High-Income Business #10kclients

Real Easy eBook, 8 Ways to Write or Repurpose Content into a Bestseller #REE8

STRATEGY #15

THE ANSWER IS..... (ANSWER QUESTIONS ON DISCUSSION BOARDS)

Discussion boards or "bulletin board" are places where you can leave messages-usually as questions- and then get responses. They are sometimes called other names such as Internet forums, message board, online forums, and discussion groups.

To find boards on your topic Google:

"best message boards for X" (X being your topic)
"best forums for X"
"best online forums"
and "discussion groups"

If you can't find one that specializes in your topic, or if you want to become more of an authority in your field by running your own discussion or forum, here is a list of the fifteen best, online platforms. http://ellenlikes.com/forumplatforms

STRATEGY #16
CHAT ABOUT IT!

Hang out in chat rooms. Chat rooms are a little different than message boards. People can leave each other messages on boards, but in chat rooms, people can talk to other people.

Chat rooms can be cost-effective for marketing. They allow you to network with others in your niche, establish you as an expert, or even book a chat room to host an event or conduct a seminar. You can use them to launch a new book, product or program, share news or get exposure you might not otherwise get. While people don't read emails as much as they used to, if you can get them to come a chat room, your message will reach them. And those who join your chats may become customers and/or fans, plus chatting can be fun.

Twitter is a great platform for chatting.

Twitter chats, also called tweet chats, tweet parties or twitter parties are easy to find and easy to set up if you want to run one.

The way you find chat parties is through hashtags. When someone sets up a chat they assign it a hash tag. Hashtags should be:

- short
- simple
- memorable
- and unique (Make sure no one else is already using it or no one may show up!)

Tweet parties are open events, but if you are going to use them, you'll want to make sure to tell as many people as possible before the scheduled party.

You can do this through tweeting, announcing it on other social-media sites, putting an announcement on your website, your blog, and your newsletter, if you have one, through an email list, and/or by reaching out to individual contacts through messenger, for instance. You can even automate it through chat bots using a program like Many Chat www.manychat.com

You can find tweet chats listed at:

Tweet Reports at: http://www.tweetreports.com posts a large list of recurring Tweet Chats on a wide range of topics including business, healthcare,, technology, social media, writing and more. They have a seven-day trial.

Twubs at: www.twubs.com posts a lengthy lists of events and updates for each days events.

You may also find chat-party information on individual companies from their websites and in the emails that they send out. Associations like Women's Speaker Association and Mommy Blog Expert do them regularly.

If you want to use tweet chats, I suggest going on a few first to see how they work. Then when you are ready, do a small one to test it out or get someone to run it for you. To manage a tweet chat, you can use Tweetdeck, TweetChat or HootSuite, My go-to guy for Twitter Chats is Gary Loper.. You can reach him through his website at: www.garyloper.com or on Twitter at: @garyloper

STRATEGY #17

LET YOUR FINGERS DO THE WALKING (PUT YOUR BOOK IN EBOOK/PDF DIRECTORIES)

eBook directories have thousands of subscribers looking for books on a wide variety of topics.

Here are a few sites and aggregate sites to get you started.

    http://www.ebookjungle.com/
    http://e-library.net/
    http://www.wisdomebooks.com/add76.html
    http://www.ebook88.com/
    http://www.feedbooks.com/
    http://bookbub.com
    http://www.ebookfreeway.com/

STRATEGY #18
COMMENTS PLEASE!

Leaving comments on high-ranking blogs, when done the right way, stand out and can capture the attention of the blog host who, in turn, can help you quickly increase your success.

To make blog commenting work for you, you must build a relationship with the host and leave comments that show you care, that you're thoughtful, and that you've actually read the post before commenting. It's also important to use good etiquette and be respectful. Being on someone's blog is like being in their home. You are a guest, and you want to respect that it's their domain.

To get off on the right foot, be sure to refer to the post and mention the author by name in your comments. Also, offer a sincere compliment if you have one to offer but avoid butt-kissing. Inauthentic compliments will turn off the host and not do you a bit of good.

In your comments, you can focus on the host, the post or both. If you're a fan of their work in general, you can tell them so. Specific examples make your comments look even more genuine.

If you are only aware of the post, see if you can answer one of more of these questions: How did it affect you? Did it motivate you? Change you? Help you? Or, inspire you? If so, let them know.

See how you can add value to the conversation. This is the most important aspect of your comments. By sharing insights, anecdotes, tips, or maybe another strategy that's worked for you, it makes the post more enjoyable and valuable for others, and most hosts will appreciate that. (A few who are insecure may see it as competition and feel threatened, but if they do, they are not people you want to build a relationship with for the long run!)

Note: Do not offer constructive criticism unless it is asked for or by first contacting the person privately and asking them if they are open to it.

STRATEGY #19
PIN IT!

Visual marketing is HOT because it works, so promote your book in Pinterest! Studies show that graphics get more interest and engagement than text, and people on Pinterest are adept at sharing content with other users. Plus, Pinterest's audience is "engaged and active" according to SocialMediaExaminer.com

You can use Pinterest to highlight your most popular books, or all your books. Whatever you think will work best for your audience.

The most popular posts on Pinterest are fashion, food, and home decorating, so if you 're writing books on these subjects, Pinterest is a natural fit for your books. But, if you're writing about other topics, you can still use Pinterest by including boards on these subjects as well, and by including them in your book marketing.

For instance, if you have a book signing and have h'ordeuves on hand, have a picture of the book with the h'ordeuves and talk about how they were made; you can even add the recipes!

You may also take advantage of group boards and form strategic partnerships with influencers in your niche.

Group boards are where you invite other users to contribute pins to a board, and it show as up in the guests followers' feed as well as your own.

Tip: You can also connect with other influencers and form strategic partnerships but don't allow too many contributors to contribute to each board. It's better to let each partner curate their own board.

Another strategy you can use with Pinterest is to thank your fans for their support after a launch or promotion, or for any assistance they give you for promoting your book, or any product, program, service, or your brand in general.

You can do this by sharing something of interest that they can use or recreate like something for free or a cake, brownies, or cookies-then share the recipe, so they can make it at home themselves. And be sure to share your thank-you pin on all social-media sites, so as many as possible can see it. Not only will your fans appreciate the gesture, but new fans will appreciate the fact that you appreciate your community, and this attracts more new fans!

You can also take pictures of your journey while writing your book and pin them as you go. Fans appreciate an interesting journey, and they love being included in the process.

If you format your book for publishing on demand (P.O.D.), you may order review copies from Amazon. Be sure to get a picture of you unwrapping the book when it arrives in the mail and another one holding it up for everyone to see! Then as you market at live events, if you do, continue to have pictures taken each time that you can pin. This will keep your book in the minds of your potential buyers and get more sales!

You can see how photos enhance the author's credibility:

One of my clients, Paul Sterling, had the opportunity to meet Marianne Williamson, and they each signed the other's book giving Paul and his book, *Argue Less Love More: 5 Communication Secrets for Couples Who Want Less Pain and More Passion*, even more credibility and authority in his field or relationships.

Another client, Dennis G. Shaver, had the opportunity to meet Shark Tank's Kevin Harrington at a conference and show Kevin his book, *The Entrepreneurial Incubator: Secrets to Getting your Invention from Mind to Market* after which Kevin became Dennis's mentor.

You can see how much more powerful their stories are by sharing pictures! And, how it invites their fans and followers to celebrate with them! Pictures like these can make all the difference in the number and depth of your relationships with your followers and fans!

And don't worry, if you haven't connected yet with any famous people, think outside the box and figure out how you can!

Invite your followers to send you pictures of themselves doing something that's in your book, like make a recipe if it's a cookbook, or exercising if it's a weight-loss book, for instance.

Or, share amazingly beautiful pictures of what inspires your vision, your mission and or your brand culture.

You also want to engage others and include them in your social media, so share their images as well and find strategic partners who can help you do it.

STRATEGY #20
THE 30% SWITCH

Take an excerpt from your book and change it by at least 30%, then upload it to Ezine Articles www.EzineArticles.com Ezine Articles is a destination site, which ranks at #6 in a list of the top fifty article directories (You can check out all fifty at: http://www.vretoolbar.com/articles/directories.php.)

But the reason I like it best is that it is very easy to use, and articles are categorized in such a way that it is easy to find what readers are looking for. Plus, it covers all the major categories: business, computers and tech, home based business, online businesses, real estate, relationship travel and leisure, finance, health and fitness, self improvement, women's interests, writing and speaking and more.

Here are two ways to change your excerpt by 30% so Ezine Article will accept it.

1. Hire someone on Fiverr to rewrite your excerpt for you.

2. Make an outline of the information, and then talk it without looking at the original text

To submit an article, join Ezine Articles at: www.EzineArticles.com. The membership is free. Here's how to submit step-by-step:

This will take you to your personal Ezine Article's Page where you click on "submit an article" under your profile picture on the left.

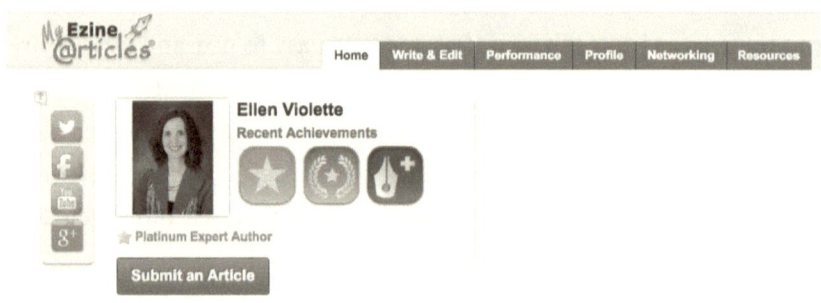

Then, just fill out the submission form

    Title,
    Category
    Summary
    Body
    Keywords

Resource Bos
  Author
  Schedule release

Preview it for formatting, grammar and spelling and submit it.

Easy, peasy!

STRATEGY #21
DISCOUNT IT!

If you put your book into KDP and plan to do a free launch or promotion, (it's called a launch on a new book, and a promotion on an already existing one) the minimum price you can sell it for is $2.99. Amazon has a pricing tool that will show you what the optimal price for your ebook is based on past performance of similar books.

If the suggested price for your book is higher than $2.99, you can discount it after your launch to $2.99. This works best when the retail price is $5.98 or higher, making it 50% off.

For instance, if your book usually sold for $7.49 then half price would be approximately $3.80. Of course, you can discount it for less if the retail is lower than $5.98 or more if the retail price is even higher.

Also, remember, that if you have a digital version and physical version, of your book, you can discount the physical version instead if it doesn't make sense to discount the digital version- in other words if the digital version is only $2.99.

You also have another option: you can do a Countdown launch or promotion, which allows you to sell your book for as low as 99 cents and still get a 70% royalty. Just be aware that to do a Countdown launch or promotion requires that your book be in Kindle for thirty days before you can do one. The reason is so that it establishes a regular price for the book. But after you meet that requirement, you can do a launch or promotion from one hour to seven days once in any ninety-day period. However, you cannot do a KDP-Select launch or promotion in the same ninety-day period as a Countdown one.

I suggest doing a free one first- especially if you are a new author and do not have a large sphere of influence because you can announce it in a lot of announcement sites that reach thousands and, sometimes, hundreds of thousands of people in your target market that you won't reach with the Countdown strategy.

So, the free launch or promotion creates a lot more buzz, and you can get hundreds of people downloading your book, which makes it a lot easier to get a #1 ranking in Kindle and on the #1 New Release List, plus it can jump start your sales by building momentum quickly. (I tested the two and found that I actually made more money from my free launch than my Countdown launch because after my two-day free launch, my book sold for $2.99 while the Countdown sold for 99 cents, and I sold about the same amount of books!

RESOURCES

Extra Bonus:

57 Ways to Market & Sell Your Book Checklist, The Fastest, Easiest Ways to Make Money with Your Book for more great ways to market your eBook at: www.BooksBusinessAbundance.com/57ways

15 Best Online Platforms

http://ellenlikes.com/forumplatforms

Article Directories

Ezine Articles
www.EzineArticles.com

Top 50 Top Directories:
http://www.vretoolbar.com/articles/directories.php

Book Formatting

- Formatting Done for you
  High-end Formatting with Inside design
  www.booksbusinessabundance.com/services
  www.fiverr.com

- Formatting Templates
  Book Design Templates
  http://ellenlikes.com/bookdesigntemplates

- Designr
  http://ellenlikes.com/designr

- Free
  http://ellenlikes.com/ebookstyles
  www.jutoh.com
  www.calibre-ebook.com
  www.smashwords.com

Cloaker

Easy Direct
http://ellenlikes.com/prettylink

eBook Directories

http://www.ebookjungle.com/
http://e-library.net/
http://www.ebookjungle.com/

http://e-library.net/
http://www.wisdomebooks.com/add76.html
http://www.ebook88.com/
http://www.feedbooks.com/
http://bookbub.com
http://www.ebookfreeway.com/

Facebook Group

www.Facebook.com/groups/selfpublishingcommunity

Graphics

www.123rf.com

Graphic Design Tool

Canva make graphics and is free, but does offer upgraded graphics for $1 each. www.Canva.com

It is very easy to use once you know how, but they do not have training so I created a special report that walks you through how to do it.

www.BooksBusinessAbundance.com/canva-graphics

Example: *How to Crush it in Business Without Crushing Your Spirit, How Entrepreneurs Can Overcome Depression and Find Success* is one of my books (an anthology) and I market it in my banner for the Facebook Group at: http://www.Facebook.com/groups/overcomingdepressionforentrepreneurs

Hosting

Hostgator http://ellenlikes.com/besthosting4u

Kindle

KDP Launches/Promotions
www.kdp.amazon.com

Kindle Planner
How to position your ebook on Kindle to become a #1 bestseller and sell more books
www.BooksBusinessAbundance.com/kindleplanner

Photography

www.twenty20.com

Podcast Guest Finders

http://myradioshowtour.com/ from Mark Bowness
http://www.podcastguests.com from Andrew Allemann
http://www.radioguestlist.com

Reviews

Getting Reviews from Amazon Reviewers
How to Get Reviews from Top Amazon Reviewers to Sell More Books with Less Effort!
http://www.BooksBusinessAbundance.com/amazon-reviewers

Twitter Expert

Gary Loper
www.garyloper.com
Twitter at: @garyloper

NEXT STEPS

1. Grab your FREE copy of 57 Ways to Market & Sell Your Book Checklist, The Fastest, Easiest Ways to Make Money with Your Book for more great ways to market your eBook at: www.BooksBusinessAbundance.com/57ways

2. PLEASE….if you enjoyed this book it would be awesome if you could leave a quick review on Amazon

3. Visit our website at www.BooksBusinessAbundance.com for more resources and to see how we can support you and your business going forward.

ABOUT ELLEN VIOLETTE

Ellen Violette is a award-winning book and business coach, multiple International #1 bestselling author, 3-time eLit award winner, former contributor to Published! Magazine, and CEO of Create a Splash. She helps entrepreneurs clarify and package their message to create instant credibility and expert status, make a big impact in the world and change lives by becoming a bestselling author and leveraging their knowledge to grow high-income businesses.

Her company is a full-service company for book services for authors and entrepreneurs, coaches, consultants, trainers, and speakers who want to become #1 bestselling authors and own their niche. It also delivers done-for-you services.

What makes Ellen unique is that she comes from a creative background as a Grammy-nominated songwriter, so she understands how to connect with an audience and say it in a unique way. For that reason she's been called "The Title Guru". She writes unique titles for her clients, guides them through the writing and publishing process, helps them become #1 bestselling authors, and shows them how to ROCK THEIR BUSINESS WITH BOOKS!

Ellen lives in San Diego with her husband, Christen Violette, a retired clinical hypnotherapist, political junkie, and her business advisor.

To learn more about Ellen and her business, go to www.booksbusinessabundance.com

www.ingramcontent.com/pod-product-compliance
Lightning Source LLC
Chambersburg PA
CBHW031922170526
45157CB00008B/3019